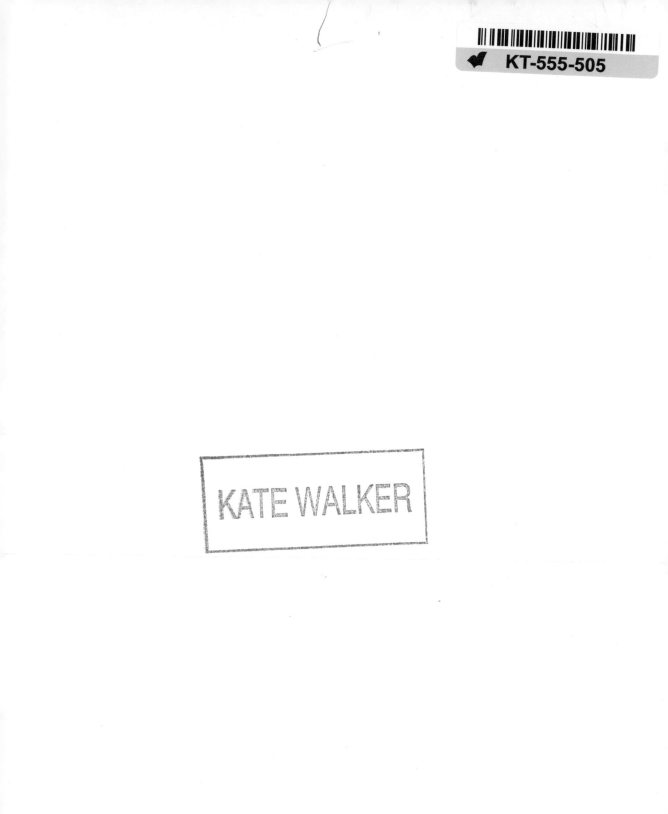

KATE WALKER

BIRD
BEHAVIOUR

Louise Dawson and Mike Langman
Introduction by Bill Oddie

HAMLYN

For Ian
From whom I have learnt so much.

First published in 1995 by Hamlyn
an imprint of Reed Consumer Books Limited
Michelin House, 81 Fulham Road, London SW3 6RB
and Auckland, Melbourne, Singapore and Toronto.

Copyright © Reed International Books Limited 1995

Text copyright © Louise Dawson 1995
Illustrations copyright © Mike Langman 1995
Photographs copyright © see page 48.

ISBN 0 600 57981 6

A CIP catalogue record for this book is available from
the British Library.

Cover photograph: Mute Swans © Richard Revels
(RSPB)
Back cover photograph: © C H Gomersall (RSPB)
Printed and bound in Hong Kong

CONTENTS

BILL ODDIE'S INTRODUCTION

Grown ups love droning on about how different – and difficult – things were when they were young. Well, when it comes to birdwatching, it's true! I was about seven when I managed to persuade my Dad to buy me my first pair of binoculars. That was over 40 years ago and there were no bird magazines or specialist optical dealers. I was lucky I didn't end up with a plastic toy pair! In fact, my first binoculars were very good and lasted for years, so Dad must have taken good advice from somewhere.

But how did I learn about how and where to go bird watching? And how did I know what I was looking at? The only identification book available was the *Observer's Book of Birds*, which didn't even have all the British birds in it, let alone pictures of them in all their plumages. The first 'modern' field guide came out in 1954 when I was 13.

I like to think, though, that by the time I became a teenager I wasn't a bad birdwatcher. So how did I do it? Well, nearly every day I used to walk to the local woods and round the golf course (watching out for flying golf balls as well as birds). Every weekend, I'd cycle to the local reservoir or persuade my Dad to give me a lift. And I'd campaign to take our family holidays in Norfolk or Devon so I could see some new birds. I spent an amazing amount of time, but looking back I probably wasted a lot too, making mistakes I could have avoided if only there'd been books like this one.

This book is about bird behaviour. What do we mean by that? Well, it's certainly not like when a schoolteacher tells the class to 'behave'. In fact, if you carried on in school like birds do, you'd probably get into quite a lot of trouble. The fact is, a large part of a bird's life is spent fighting, hunting and showing off to the opposite sex. Behaving quite badly, in fact! But there's more to it than that and you can read about it here. Even better, you can go out and watch it actually happening. The brilliant thing about studying bird behaviour is that you don't have to go far to see it, and there is still lots of fascinating stuff to be discovered. It is perfectly possible that a young ornithologist could find out something new!

This is what makes birdwatching such a wonderful hobby. It's not just about identifying species and keeping lists. That is only the start. Birdwatching is an interest for life. I'm still at it – never give it up.

Bill Oddie

INTRODUCTION

This book is all about what birds do and why they do it. Experts call it 'bird behaviour'. Understanding what's going on in a bird's life brings birdwatching alive and makes a day out even more exciting. You'll start to see birds doing things you've never noticed before – and you'll be amazed at their behaviour.

Even if you could identify all the birds in the world (and there probably isn't anyone who can), you wouldn't have much fun seeing them if you didn't have a clue what they were doing when you watched them. Understanding why birds do what they do and learning to spot when they are doing it is probably the most fascinating part of birdwatching. And as birds are always on the go, there's always plenty to see.

Whether you're an absolute beginner or whether you know a bit about birds already, this book will help you see even the birds in your garden or around town very differently. After this book, I hope that birds will never look quite the same to you again.

Louise Dawson

Willow warbler singing

A BIRD'S LIFE

Birds live everywhere in the world - in towns and cities, over the sea, on the tops of mountains, and in the coldest and the hottest parts of the world. There are around 9,000 different kinds of bird alive today. As a group of animals they are very successful.

The power of flight

Flight is the secret of success for birds – it was the envy of man for centuries. Being able to fly means that birds can go virtually any-where, and fast. Travel by air is easy for birds and many have taken advantage of it to migrate huge distances. It has also helped birds reach places physically out of reach to other animals.

Because they can fly, thousands of seabirds can nest on rocky cliff faces around the UK coastline during May and June. The sheer drop to the sea and the crashing waves offer protection from predators.

Birds are adaptable

Birds are also successful because they adapt to change. The starling is one of the most adaptable birds. It originally lived in Europe and western Asia, but has done really well wherever it has been introduced in the world.

The secret is food – starlings are really insect-eaters, but will eat many different foods to survive, including berries and fruit, frogs and lizards. You may have watched them in winter, strutting about garden lawns, poking about for hidden fat, grey grubs called leatherjackets. And they will visit bird tables and hang off nut feeders too.

Like all birds, they must decide what is the best food to eat at any time. They won't always eat the nearest and most convenient food. They have to consider what is going to do them the most good. Male starlings will eat barley in winter, but females must eat lots of small insects and spiders to be in good condition to breed in the spring.

Food is energy

Everything birds do uses energy and that energy comes from the food they eat. Choosing the right food is very important, especially for flight, which uses a lot of energy.

A starling's year: listen out for the starling's song in January.

Starlings begin nest-hunting in late winter.

Eggs are laid in spring (from mid-April). There may be two clutches.

Archaeopteryx is the oldest known bird, from which today's birds have evolved. It lived 150 million years ago. Scientists have used fossils to build up a picture of what this feathered dinosaur must have looked like.

But for most birds, being able to fly is worth the extra effort. Of course, birds can save energy. At night, when they are not eating, many birds huddle up together to roost. By sharing their body warmth with other birds, they spend less of their own energy on keeping warm.

Starlings gather in huge roosts at dusk in winter. Roosting birds may also pass on and receive information about good places to feed from other birds.

Birds' lives change with the seasons, except in the tropics. When it's warm, there is plenty of food; when it's much colder, food is scarce and life is hard. What birds do is very closely timed to the seasons.

Breeding, moulting (growing new feathers) and migration all use lots of energy. But breeding uses the most and so birds must breed when it's warm and food is plentiful. For the best start in life, young starlings must hatch in May when caterpillars and grubs are in good supply.

The same but different

Like all birds, a starling's life is closely timed to the seasons. Starlings all behave in a broadly similar way, but every bird is an individual and will do things slightly differently from other starlings.

Each individual starling will be faced every day with its own choices to make, such as where to look for food, what to eat, where to nest or which bird to have as a mate. And so it is for all birds. And that is what makes the study of bird behaviour so fascinating.

The eggs hatch in early May when there is plentiful insect food.

Adults begin moulting when their families are reared. Then they fatten up for the winter.

Some starlings stay near their breeding area; others migrate.

GETTING AROUND

Man has envied birds' power of flight for centuries. Birds' lives are geared up for flying and their bodies are made to be good at it and they are successful because they can fly.

Flight is a fast and easy way to travel. Finding food is easier because birds can search bigger areas in less time and they can find food that is out of reach to other animals. In the sky, birds can escape from from many predators and, because flight means birds can cover big distances, they can migrate.

Many birds have a winter and a summer home, which means they can make the most of two places during the year. When food is scarce in winter, some birds migrate to where there is more of it and spend winter there. And when it warms up in spring and there is more food where they came from, they can fly back to breed.

Flapping two wings is hard work and it uses up lots of energy. Without a specially adapted body, birds would never leave the ground! They have special breathing and blood systems for moving lots of oxygen and energy to where they're needed, fast. They have large hearts and big, powerful lungs.

But they also need to be light enough to take off! They have specially adapted bones that are light but amazingly strong – some are specially honeycombed inside to be lighter. Birds have had to make sacrifices too, though. To fly, birds have had to do without hands. Their hands are adapted as wings so they use their feet and bills to feed with.

Feathers are vital for flight. All birds have feathers – those that fly have special feathers for the job. Birds must be able to take off, stay in the air by flapping and gliding, and land without crashing. When a bird flaps its wings the downward push creates the lift that keeps the bird up in the air, and other wing movement creates thrust to move the bird forward.

Flapping during flight uses lots of energy, so birds can save energy by gliding. Most birds do this, but the bigger the wingspan, the easier gliding is. In general, small birds are agile fliers with fast wingbeats, whereas large birds find it harder to dodge obstacles and change direction quickly, but are much better at gliding and soaring.

The mute swan is Britain's heaviest flying bird. It needs a long, clear 'runway' across water, using its feet to run along the water until it lifts off.

The ostrich has lost the ability to fly but escapes enemies by running instead. Adults can reach speeds of 30mph. Another large bird, the cassowary, chooses fight instead of flight and is very aggressive!

gave it up because they had no need to fly! Some birds living on remote islands had no enemies and simply didn't need to fly to live. This made them very easy to catch and kill and sadly, many of these birds were virtually wiped out when humans discovered them. Either they were killed by pets and pests brought to the islands, or they were hunted to extinction. The dodo and the great auk, both large, docile and easy to catch, are now extinct. Others have been rescued just in time. The kakapo is a weird, big, flightless parrot from New Zealand. Once killed by cats and rats introduced by settlers, it has been saved in the nick of time by conservationists.

The long wing feathers furthest away from this blue tit's body are called primary feathers. Those nearest its body are called secondaries and coverts and give the bird lift in flight, keeping it airborne.

The fastest fliers are ducks, which can move very fast indeed. The eider duck's direct flight is the fastest recorded. Hummingbirds have the fastest wingbeats – at least 90 every second! Sparrowhawks have shortish wings and long tails for speed and easy movement in woodland. But the award for the fastest bird goes to the peregrine. Its steep dive in the air onto prey (called a 'stoop') has clocked an amazing 110mph!

To fly or not to fly?

Some birds cannot fly. For some, being big is more useful than being able to fly. The ostrich, rhea, emu, cassowary and penguins cannot fly. For penguins, it was more important to be able to be heavy with fat to survive the cold and be fast and agile in the water. Their wings have become underwater flippers and they have extra fat to keep warm.

Not all birds gave up flying to be good swimmers or faster on their feet. Some

About feathers

Feathers are what make birds different – no other creatures have them. Birds use them for lots of things: to blend in with their surroundings (called camouflage); to show off to a mate or a rival; to keep warm and as waterproofing. Feathers also give birds their shape and their colour.

Feathers come in different shapes and sizes – different feathers have different jobs to do. They can be as long as 165 cm, as in the case of the crested argus pheasant of south-east Asia, and over 12.5 cm wide. The smallest feathers are on birds' eyelids!

All feathers have a purpose. Those on the body and the head are called contour feathers: these give shape and outline. Downy feathers are soft and fluffy and form an underwear layer to keep in the warmth. There are other feathers, called plumes, which keep birds warm. Many birds have bristles around their beaks, eyes and nostrils and these help in finding food. And there are different kinds of flight feathers and tail feathers too.

Feathers are thought to have developed from the scales of reptile ancestors, but no-one knows for sure. Feathers are made from keratin – a tough substance that also makes up the skin of reptiles. Your nails also have keratin in them, which makes them tough but also light and strong.

Next time you find a feather, study it closely. You'll see that it has a stiff quill which runs

Where there's water, birds will bathe in it. Puddles, ponds, bird baths and even upturned dustbin lids all make great baths for garden birds such as this blackbird.

up the centre. The rest of the feather (the soft part) is called the vane. The vane is made up of lots of barbs, attached to the quill. Take a close look at these barbs through a magnifying glass and you'll see that each barb has two sets of fine barbules branching out from it. Each barbule has a cup and hook (called a barbicel) at its end. Barbicels work rather like a zip does and help 'knit' the feather together. With use, feathers get ruffled and the barbicels come undone from each other. For the feather to work properly, they must be 'zipped' back neatly into place. Birds do this by preening.

This jay is 'anting'. With wings spread and tail twisted sideways, it picks up ants and puts them on its wings. No-one knows exactly why, but the acid ants make helps rid the jay of lice living in its feathers.

Feather care

Feathers are vital for a bird's healthy life, so they must be kept in good condition. Birds do this by preening, moulting, bathing, dusting, sunning and anting. Birds spend time every day preening to comb the barbs of the feathers together. They do this by running the beak the length of the feather, using it to 'zip' the barbs into position. At the same time, the beak is also used to pick off any parasites – unwelcome guests that might be living in the bird's feathers.

Most birds have a special gland at the base of their backs, just above the tail, called a 'preen gland'. It makes a special oil, which birds use to coat their feathers. It's especially important for water birds, which must use oil to keep their feathers waterproof.

Moulting

Feathers wear out and have to be replaced. Birds shed them every now and then and grow new ones. This is called moulting. All birds moult at least once a year. Usually they do it after the breeding season but before migration, when it's best to have brand new feathers. Ducks, geese and swans lose all their flight feathers at once, which means they can't fly for a while. They are vulnerable at this time and have dull, brownish plumage to hide from predators.

Bath time

Most birds bathe, even when it's cold. They don't soak, but ruffle their feathers so that they can be wetted, then they splash to shower themselves all over with droplets of water. Even waterbirds, such as mute swans, bathe. Some birds bathe in the rain. Parrots stand and take a rain shower with their feathers ruffled and tail and wings outstretched. Airborne birds plunge-dive to bathe. Swifts, swallows, owls, kingfishers and hummingbirds will all dip into water for a quick bath. After bathing, birds find a safe place to preen. The wet feathers help to spread the preen oil.

Sunning can help 'iron out' twists in a bird's feathers. This blackbird is 'panting' to lose heat in the hot sun.

Buzzards moult their feathers gradually. This bird will soon grow a new flight feathers to replace the ones it has lost.

Cormorants are thought to hold their wings outstretched to dry their feathers.

Waterbirds preen their feathers to be waterproof. They transfer oil from the preen gland on their back to the rest of their feathers.

out in just few minutes. Perhaps they simply enjoy it!

Walking, hopping and climbing

Many birds spend more time walking, hopping or climbing than flying. The first birds were probably animals that climbed and clambered through the trees and used their wings to glide between one tree and another. In general, birds that spend most of their time in trees tend to hop along the ground, whereas those that nest and feed on the ground get around by walking.

Birds that live in trees need a good sense of balance for climbing and clinging to twigs and branches. Perching birds (or 'passerines', as they are known) such as our great tit, robin, blackbird, rook and pied wagtail, can 'lock' their feet in position around a branch to hold on when roosting.

The best climbers are birds that feed on tree trunks. Woodpeckers and treecreepers have to be able to cling to an upright trunk and have specially adapted claws and tail feathers so that they can do so. Both have special, stiff feathers in their tail. They can hop up and down the trunk, pressing their stiff tails against the trunk for

Cleaning by dust

Many birds bathe in dust. House sparrows often do this. There are birds of dry, dusty country, such as sandgrouse and bustards, which only bathe in dust and not in water. They scrape with their feet and shuffle with their wings so their feathers become full of dust. Dusting helps dislodge parasites.

Sunbathing

Some birds sunbathe just to warm up. But birds sunbathe when they are already hot, so there must be another reason for it. The feathers of large birds become bent when soaring and sunbathing can straighten them

A kingfisher takes a bath by plunge-diving into a river.

The great spotted woodpecker has strong, sharp curved claws, powerful leg muscles and a stiff tail. It needs a strong grip on the trunk, especially when hammering in search of food.

Swimming and diving

Birds must be specially adapted for life in the water. Many birds only use water for drinking or bathing in and would quickly drown if they fell in because their feathers would become water-logged and pull them under.

Herons live near the water's edge and use their long legs to stand clear of the water.

For a truly watery life, birds need to be waterproof and be able to stay afloat. The feathers of waterbirds are specially adapted to enable them to do this. Overlapping feathers trap air which helps keep a bird buoyant. Most birds have very light bones and very big lungs, both of which help keep them afloat.

For birds that spend a lot of time diving or swimming underwater, the ability to sink is more useful than being a good floater! So diving birds have heavier bones with smaller air sacs than land birds. Grebes, divers and diving ducks can force air out of their feathers and lungs to help them sink. Cormorants can waterlog their feathers, which is thought to help them reach deeper waters to feed.

Many waterbirds have webbed feet to give more push in water. Razorbills, puffins and guillemots use their narrow wings to 'fly' underwater and their tail and feet to steer.

support. Coming down a tree trunk isn't as easy! Even tree-dwellers like treecreepers and woodpeckers can only shuffle down. Nuthatches can scale the bark head-first.

Birds that spend most of their time on the ground need stronger legs and they tend to have stronger or fewer toes. Some of the best runners have very few toes: the ostrich has only two.

Marsh birds have big feet with long toes which work a bit like snowshoes, spreading the weight over a wider area so they don't sink when walking on lily pads and mats of floating plants.

Penguins are the most adapted for swimming of any bird.

BIRD SENSES

Birds have much the same senses as you and I: they see, hear, smell and feel. Their senses are also finely tuned for life in the air. For flight they need good balance, a keen sense of touch to feel the air over their feathers, and excellent eyesight.

Birds behave in two ways: some things they do by instinct (as if programmed); others they have to learn. Birds of the same species have the same instinctive behaviour: gannets dive for fish, but blue tits do not. But birds can learn things from each other. When one blue tit discovered how to break open the top of a milk bottle, other blue tits learnt by watching. Blue tits do not instinctively know how to raid milk bottles – they learn it from other blue tits.

Good sight is vital for fast flight. Birds' eyes focus twice as well as ours – they can see far away things as clearly as really close objects. They can see with both eyes separately, as well as by using both together. Most birds have their eyes on the sides of their head, which makes it easy to see all round and spot danger, but makes forward vision more difficult.

Although birds see in colour, they are thought to be more sensitive to the colours of the foods that they eat, so that flowers that are red, yellow or orange stand out to them. In a world-wide survey of plants that use birds to spread their seeds, five in every 10 had mainly red flowers. Birds are also sensitive to ultra-violet light, which may help migrants work out where the sun is on dull days.

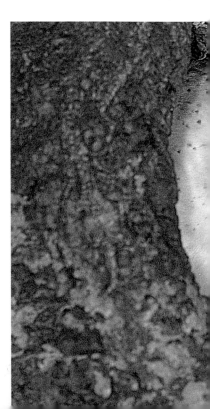

The woodpecker finch of the Galapagos Islands is one of very few tool-using birds. It uses its bill to prise off bark to expose insect holes. Then, if it can't reach its prey using its bill alone, it fetches a cactus spine and uses it to prise the insect out. The grey flycatcher of the Serengeti, Tanzania, also uses twigs like this.

Colour is used by many birds to send messages. To a male robin, the red breast of another robin triggers a battle for territory.

Red is such a powerful signal during the breeding season that robins have been known to attack red jumpers on washing lInes!

Birds hear as well as humans, but some hear better than others. They use their ears to hear other birds' songs and calls, find their prey, detect predators and find their way in the dark. They are better at pinpointing sound than we are and can detect lower sounds than we can. Parrots, ducks and owls have especially good hearing.

Some birds have a much better sense of smell than others. Honeyguides can sniff out bees' nests and seabirds, such as shearwaters, albatrosses, fulmars and storm petrels, can smell food over long distances.

Touch, taste and temperature are also important senses. The male mallee fowl makes a compost-heap nest and uses the warmth it makes to incubate its eggs. It uses its bill as a thermometer to check the heap isn't too hot.

Birds can taste their food, but are less fussy than us - we have lots more taste buds! Woodpeckers feel for food in holes with their tongues. Waders have specially sensitive

A barn owl's face funnels sound into ears hidden in the face. One ear is tilted higher than the other so the owl can pinpoint sound more accurately.

Hunting birds have their eyes at the front of their heads which gives them good forward vision to catch their prey. A hovering kestrel (top) can keep its head motionless in one position to watch for prey, while the rest of its body moves.

The woodcock (above) has eyes on the sides of its head, near the top to spot danger from all around. To see in front, it tilts its head and looks with one eye.

The grey heron's eyes (left) are at the front of its head and can see fish with both eyes at the same time, which helps it judge position.

Parrots like this grey parrot have their eyes on the sides of their head. Like the woodcock, they cock their head sideways to look around.

bills for finding worms in sand and mud, and finches can 'hear' through their legs with special organs that detect sounds too low-pitched for our ears. Scientists think migrating birds can sense the earth's magnetic field and detect changes in atmospheric pressure.

Birds at night

Very little is known about what birds do at night - it's too dark for people to study them! But new study techniques are giving away some secrets. It is not only owls that are active at night: many birds we see during the day are also busy at night. In Europe, robins may sing until it's almost dark and flocks of swifts rise high in the sky, screeching as they go – they are believed to roost on the wing.

Many waterbirds will feed at night if the light is good enough. Estuary birds feed when the tide uncovers

A tawny owl's flight is silent – its feathers are specially adapted to make no wind noise – vital for swooping down on prey undetected.

rich muddy feeding grounds. If the tide is just right for feeding when it's dark, wading birds will carry on feeding.

Many birds migrate at night, but why is not fully understood: they may be using the pattern of the stars to help them find their way, or they may migrate at night so that they can avoid predation and make full use of the daylight to feed.

But why be active at night at all? Why aren't all birds out and about only during the day? By making use of all 24 hours in the day birds compete less with each other – it's as if different species are doing different shifts during the 24 hours. For example, in the Camargue Marshes of southern France, night herons – thought to be dawn and dusk feeders – were seen feeding in the middle of the night, out of the way of the little egrets and purple herons which feed during the twilight hours and by day.

Another reason for night life is it allows birds to eat food that isn't available by day. The kiwi and woodcock feed on worms at night, when worms are nearer to the surface of the soil and easier to find. Tubenosed seabirds also feed at night, when marine creatures come to the surface of the sea.

In the dark, birds can be safer from predators than during daylight. Nesting colonies of petrels and shearwaters are busy at night, but the adults get ready to feed at sea as soon as dawn breaks. Nesting by night gives them some protection from predators such as gulls.

Birds active at night rest during the day.

The kiwi is the only bird known to use smell to find food in the ground - handy, because it feeds in the dark. It sniffs out earthworms with a long, probing bill that has nostrils at the tip, not on top like most birds.

Some hide in thick cover in trees or on the ground; others, such as the nightjar and woodcock, are camouflaged, which allows them to blend into their surroundings.

Birds active by night need specially adapted senses to help them find their way around. Tawny owls use darkness and silent flight to hunt. Their vision is good, but is only 2½ times more sensitive to light than a human's. But they do have excellent 3-D vision, which makes solid objects stand out, so prey is easy to spot against a background.

All eyes must have some light by which to see. Even owls cannot see in complete darkness. The oilbird of Venezuela, however, lives in complete darkness in caves. It has big eyes which help it search for fruit at night outside the cave, but in the complete darkness of the cave it uses its own radar - a kind of echo-location similar to that used by bats. The bird sends out a series of clicks and uses the rebounding echoes to work out exactly where it is in the blackness of the cave. Some cave swiftlets of southern India and southeast Asia also use echo-location.

Our nightjar is crepuscular (which means active at dawn and dusk). It eats night-flying insects, especially moths.

During spring and summer, robins can be mistaken for nightingales because they often sing late into the evening and sometimes during the night.

FOOD AND FEEDING

Birds must eat to live. Finding, eating and storing food takes up a lot of time and influences how a bird behaves.

Do birds know what to eat and how to feed when they are born or do they have to learn it? Birds probably feed partly by instinct and partly by learning. Hand-reared blue tits that have never seen their natural food, prefer the same food as wild tits. Hand-reared kestrels can pounce on live mice and kill them with a bite to the neck, but they have to learn not to kill a dead mouse! Young birds get better at finding food with practice. Parent birds continue to feed their fledglings while they learn.

Sometimes, conditions are so bad that birds do nothing but feed just to survive. Tits must feed all through the day in winter to survive the night. After winter, there is more food and birds have time to breed.

The right meal is important. A tit that takes all day to find a caterpillar won't live long. Birds have to make the best use of their time and of the food they find. Birds eat to get the best and biggest meal for the least

Wood pigeons and other birds need to drink, but the amount they need depends on how hot or cold it is and how much water their food contains.

effort. For a plover, a big worm is better than a small worm – but if the worm is too big to handle, the plover will waste time and energy struggling to eat it. Medium-sized worms are the best bet and flocks of plovers and lapwings know where they are in the soil. By probing at the right depth, they can find medium-sized worms most of the time.

Some birds eat a wide range of food. Spotted flycatchers eat flying insects – there can be plenty around one minute, and very few the next, so they must adapt quickly. When insects are flying, flycatchers make sorties to catch bees, wasps, flies and butterflies from a perch; when it's cooler and insects stop flying, flycatchers may search leaves and twigs for aphids and spiders.

Birds also store food for harder times. Kestrels sometimes hide food during the day and return to eat it in the evening. This means they weigh less during the day, which may make flight easier, and they have full stomachs at night when they need to keep warm. Jays bury acorns and remember where they've hidden them.

Yellow wagtails catch insects disturbed by cattle as they graze in summer meadows.

As they bury more than they need, the uneaten ones grown into oak trees.

Birds often have to feed with others and fighting for their fair share means less time for eating. When flocks gather around food, competition can be fierce. Birds that are part of a regular flock are more ordered: they may have a 'pecking order' where birds take turns to feed.

Feeding in a flock offers more protection from predators and there are more eyes on the look-out for danger, which means more time for eating. They can also see what other birds have found. For example, the sight of terns diving tells others where a shoal of fish has been found.

Where prey gathers in large numbers, it makes sense for birds to feed together. White pelicans herd shoals of fish into a smaller and smaller area by swimming in a half-circle, then they scoop them up into their big bills.

Birds and other animals

Many birds feed near to other animals. Robins wait for gardeners to uncover worms. Gulls, auks, shearwaters and phalaropes gather in the shallow parts of the Bering Sea to feed where grey whales have stirred the mud on the seabed, bringing marine animals to the surface. The honeyguide has a partnership with honey badgers. This bird is related to woodpeckers and eats bees, their larvae and beeswax. They can smell wax from a distance, but they can't open tough bees' nest without the help of a honey badger. Having found a nest, the bird finds a badger, calls to it and leads it to the nest. The badger then tears open the nest with its strong claws and eats the honey and grubs. When it has finished, the honeyguide feeds on what is left.

In Africa, cattle egrets gather in fields with wildebeests to eat insects and other small creatures disturbed by their feet.

The bill of a greenfinch is short and stout, which makes it ideal for cracking open hard seeds.

The curlew uses its long, down-curved beak to probe deep into mud for worms on the coast and in wet grassland.

Sparrowhawks and other meat-eaters have hook-shaped bills for tearing the flesh of their prey.

A ruby-throated hummingbird has a fine bill which it uses to probe into flowers to sip sweet nectar.

A green woodpecker's bill is long and strong for hammering into dead wood to uncover food below.

The shoveler dabbles on the surface of fresh water, using its bill to sift food particles.

In any habitat, no two kinds of bird will eat exactly the same food. Two species may eat some similar things, but they won't have to fight for all the food. The way one bird can live alongside another by making its living in a different way, is called its 'niche'.

Plant-eaters

Leaves and sap contain less energy value than animal foods and are also difficult to digest. Only a few birds are adapted to eat leaves. These include swans, geese, grouse and some ducks. The kakapo parrot, pigeons, coots and the ostrich eat leaves, but they eat other food as well. The leaves are ground up in the bird's gizzard (a special grinding bag in the throat) to release the sap.

Grazing geese flocks spend most of the day feeding, picking off grasses and grinding them. They select the best shoots to make the most of a poor diet. Other parts of plants are very good foods and many birds feed on fruit for their sugar and seeds for their starch content.

Seed-eaters

Many birds eat seeds. Some are pests to farmers because they gather in flocks to feed on the seeds of wheat or rice. The kernel is the part that is eaten and it's usually protected by a tough husk or shell, which must be removed. Many seed-eaters are skilled at removing the husk before swallowing the seed. They have short, strong bills and strong jaw muscles for crushing seeds.

The hawfinch has the most powerful bill and jaw muscles of all of the finches. It eats mainly beech and hornbeam seeds, but it can crack open the tough stones of cherries. Nuthatches and great tits have smaller bills and hammer or chisel seeds to open them. But seeds are seasonal and birds have to eat something else when they run out, store their food, or move to where there is more food. Bearded tits switch to eating insects during the summer, while jays store acorns in autumn.

Goldfinches are seed-eaters but have finer, more pointed bills than most seed-eaters. They are the perfect shape for teasing out the small seeds of teasel heads.

Worms are a rich protein source for blackbirds. Song thrushes break open snail shells on a stone or 'anvil'. Broken pieces of shell are a tell-tale sign to look for.

Hummingbirds are perfectly designed for hovering in front of flowers to feed.

The crossbill is a specialist feeder. It uses the crossed tips of its bill to open cones, but it can eat berries and insects too.

Fruit and nectar eaters

In the tropics, where trees can fruit all year round, there are birds that eat only fruit, including some toucans, hornbills, oilbirds, and parrots. Many trees use birds to spread their seeds. The birds are attracted to the fleshy fruit, eat it and spit out the seed or stone inside, which falls to the ground to grow into a new tree.

Birds have become adapted to dealing with fruit and trees have evolved to be attractive to birds. Fruit is always in good supply in the tropics and so birds have plenty of time to attract a mate, court, build a nest and rear young. Some tropical fruit-eaters do this in real style! But fruit is not as good as animal food and many fruit-eaters feed their young on insects.

Some birds sip nectar – the sweet juice that some flowers produce to attract birds and flying insects. Warblers and tits visit plants occasionally for a drink, but hummingbirds, honeycreepers, sunbirds and honeyeaters are specialists. These birds live mostly in the tropics and sub-tropics where the climate is warm enough for plants to produce nectar all year round. In countries where the climate is more seasonal, nectar-eaters top up with fruit and berries.

Insect-eaters

Insects are plentiful and live all over the world, which makes them good food for birds. Swallows and swifts eat nothing else, while many birds eat them occasionally. Birds that eat insects also tend to eat spiders, snails, worms and other small animals. Insect-eaters collect their food in different ways and they have bills to suit. Tits and warblers use their little bills as tweezers to pick small insects off leaves and twigs. Swifts and swallows scoop up flying insects in their

wide mouths as they fly. Woodpeckers and woodcreepers have chisel-like bills for exposing insects in wood.

Many insects are camouflaged to hide from their predators. They may be coloured to blend in with their backgrounds; other insects taste foul and use bright colours to warn would-be predators that they are not worth eating. Some insects have adopted bright colours to make birds think that they do taste bad, and it works! Tits are known to remember nasty-tasting insects up to a year after trying to eat them.

Waterbirds

Many of the world's birds live in or on water. Some live in freshwater rivers and lakes; some depend on the sea. Others move from one to the other. Ducks live in fresh water, salt water and on land. They eat a wide range of foods and live their lives in different ways. There are broad groups of ducks: dabbling or surface-feeding ducks, and diving ducks. Mallards and shovelers are dabbling ducks. They use their bills to sift small bits of animal and plant food from shallow water. Diving ducks include long-tailed ducks, scot-

ers and eiders, which spend much of their time at sea where they eat mussels, crabs, sea urchins and slow-moving fish.

The sawbills (mergansers, smews and goosanders) have serrated edges to their beaks which they use when they dive to catch fish, crabs and other crustaceans.

Herons, storks, ibises and other long-legged birds use stealth. They stand on land or in shallow water and stalk their prey or wait for it to come to them.

The black heron is sometimes called the 'umbrella bird'. It spreads its wings over its head to make a shady refuge which unsuspecting fish swim into, only to become the heron's next meal!

The little grebe is a good diver.

The wood stork gropes for prey with an open bill, while the yellow-billed stork and spoonbills sweep their open bills from side to side, clamping down on any morsel that fails to escape.

The black-browed albatross spends most of its life at sea.

Seabirds

The world's oceans are the home of nearly 300 different birds. Some live all their lives at sea, coming to land only to breed. Others use the sea only occasionally as a place to hunt over coastal waters. The richest areas of the sea occur where currents meet and mix. Some seabirds use the ocean surface, others dive in shallow water while others can dive to a depth of 100 m in open water. There are no entirely vegetarian seabirds – all eat animals, mainly fish.

Frigatebirds are flying acrobats and they pick prey from the surface of the sea, catch flying fish or rob other seabirds. Skimmers skim the lower half of their bills (called the lower mandible) through the surface of the water, finding food by touch. Petrels, gulls and fulmars settle to feed. Fulmars peck at the surface. Pelicans use their big, floppy pouches as a net to scoop fish from the shallows. Gannets and boobies plunge-dive from the air towards fish. Penguins and others chase their prey underwater. By feeding in different ways, the birds are not competing for the same food.

and spending winter on shores and estuaries where there are big stretches of mud. These rich feeding grounds contain amazing numbers of ragworms, crustaceans and other creatures. The numbers are highest in autumn, falling in late winter, when the cold kills many invertebrates. Waders' bills are the perfect size for what they eat. This means that several species can feed in one small area of mudflat at the same time because they are all eating different things. Sandpipers have short, thin

Wading birds

Waders run and wade and many species have long legs. They include oystercatchers, avocets, stilts, plovers and sandpipers. Many are long-distance migrants, breeding in the Arctic

Waders feeding together

bills to probe just under the surface; plovers have short, stout bills to peck on the surface. Turnstones lever stones over to expose animals underneath. Phalaropes swim around picking up tiny creatures on or just underneath the water. Curlews, snipes, godwits and woodcocks thrust their bills deep into sand and mud in search of worms.

But, in winter, waders can only feed when the tide is out. Poor weather can make feeding difficult, so waders will feed at night if the tides are right and there is enough light. Some waders move inland in hard weather.

Hunters

Hunting birds include raptors (eagles, hawks and falcons) and owls. Their lives depend on them being able to spot prey, chase it, catch it and kill it. They must also hunt in the right places to find prey. They appear to learn this from their parents and stay with them longer than other birds.

Predators prefer an easy meal and will take sick, weak or injured prey if it's easy to catch. Predators have good eyesight and hearing for hunting, and most catch their prey with long, sharp talons. Over generations, hunters have become better at hunting, but prey have become better at hiding and defence. Prey are alert, quick and often armed, so hunting can be dangerous. Hunters must

Gulls like this herring gull are much more common inland than they were 30 years ago. In winter, they move inland to scavenge on rubbish tips.

use surprise, silence and speed and try to get really close before pouncing.

The peregrine has the fastest strike of any bird. It attacks in flight in open country, descending on flying birds in a steep mid-air dive at great speed, often killing prey outright or dragging it to the ground.

Sparrowhawks can't hunt in the same way in woodland: they fly low over the ground with a flap and glide action, zipping over a hedge or round a bush to ambush small birds. Kestrels watch the ground from a tree

Vultures on the plains of East Africa quickly gather at a carcass and nothing goes to waste.

The osprey usually swoops down and catches fish from the water's surface, but sometimes plunges right in after its meal.

or telegraph pole look-out, or hover in mid-air and watch for tell-tale movements below. Harriers 'quarter' the ground, gently gliding and flapping one way, then turning round and going the other, to search a new area of ground from above.

Different hunters eat a different range of food, so there is little overlap in diet. To catch big prey requires powerful feet and legs, such as eagles have. Catching slippery fish requires rough, grippy feet like those of ospreys. But others eat a wider range of food. The hobby eats big insects such as dragon-flies as well as birds, and kestrels will eat beetles as well as small mammals.

Scavengers

All hunters prefer an easy meal and eating dead meat or the remains of another's dinner is one way to do it. Others scavenge for a living. It's easier than hunting, is less danger-ous and ensures nothing goes to waste. Many birds, especially crows and gulls, scavenge occasionally and will eat dead meat (called carrion) if they can find it. Kites are well-known scavengers. But true scav-engers, like the vultures, have to roam far and wide on the look-out for food. Their big wings allow them to soar on warm air cur-rents over huge distances, so that they can search the ground from high in the sky. A vulture that drops down to the ground is quickly spotted by other circling vultures. A

real pecking order has evolved between species at a carcass. Different vulture species behave in different ways and all get their share of food without directly compet-ing with each other.

Pirates

Pirates specialise in stealing food that other birds have just caught. 'Kleptoparasitism' is another word for this robbing behaviour. Food-stealing is a habit that birds have adopted in some areas but not in others. In some parts of the Antarctic, skuas steal from blue-eyed shags; in others, they don't. Even birds of prey will steal food from smaller birds if they can't find food themselves.

Food-stealing is common in seabird colonies, where adults constantly bring food for their young, and provide an easy target for marauding skuas and large gulls nesting nearby. In the tropics, frigatebirds are expert food-stealers.

Great skuas are powerful birds and will chase other seabirds, such as this puffin, until they give up their catch of fish.

COMMUNICATION

Birds are great communicators: their calls, songs and displays are a bird language that shows other birds what they will do next or how they feel.

Starlings in a flock which is about to take off send signals to each other. Each bird crouches ready to spring into the air and fly away. The crouch is a signal to other starlings to get ready to fly.

A goose that spots danger shows its alarm by straightening its neck, which alerts the rest of the feeding flock.

Displays are special signals that all birds of the same species understand. They are a sign language for how birds feel, but the signs do not have the precise meaning of words. Displays, calls and songs are used to say 'this is my territory – go away!' and 'I want a mate', but the message is not always clear.

A robin shows off his red breast to a rival by putting his head back to show more of his red feathers. It is a sign of aggression, but it also makes him easy to attack, so he is also vulnerable.

Threatening displays make a fight less likely because both birds are likely to back-off to avoid injury. Gulls make a threatening display by approaching each other with their necks stretched, bills pointing down, and their wings held out. This means 'I may attack – watch out!'.

For birds that live together, fighting is pointless, so they tend to display to cool a squabble. If one bird shows aggression, the other may give in by hiding its bill and squatting to look smaller and less threatening.

Displays are also used to attract a mate. These displays often have bits of attacking and submissive behaviour mixed in together.

A male peacock is much more spectacular to look at than a female. He fans his eye-marked feathers into a circle of colour to attract his mate.

To mate, the two birds have to overcome their natural urge to attack each other.

Display helps to build trust between them. Formal displays that are recognised 'language' by birds of a species have evolved from everyday bits of behaviour. Signalling is helped by a bird's body – plumes of colourful feathers, patches of bare skin and the way they are used all help to send messages.

Male ducks have a speculum in their wing. This is a bright patch of colour that shows in flight. Look closely at drake mallards and teals and you will see it.

In some species, the female chooses her mate by his plumage. Over time, the males of these species have evolved to look more and more showy. This is called sexual selection

A goldeneye drake throws his head back over his back and calls to display to a female.

and birds of paradise, lyrebirds, cotingas and pheasants are spectacular examples.

Birds also sing and call to each other. Songs can be simple or very complex. Birds don't have a 'voice box' like humans': the voice is made low down in the throat and is changed by a bird's tongue and mouth.

One group of birds, the songbirds, have very well-developed voices, although not all of them are tuneful! The reed warbler sings two tunes at once.

Songs advertise territory and they are often quite musical. Bird song varies through the year. Males use it to attract females, but also to warn other males not to enter their

Each dunlin flying in a twisting, turning flock like this must carefully watch its neighbours to see which way the flock will go next.

territory – so song is a love and hate message at the same time.

Most birds sing at the start of the breeding season; some stop after finding a mate, and others go on singing throughout the nesting period. When breeding is over, birds moult and cannot fly so they must lie low until their new feathers grow. In autumn, after moulting, many birds sing again for a while. Migrants may sing before they migrate.

At the start of the breeding season, males sing all day until they attract a mate. The male will carry on singing throughout the season, but will sing less once his mate is nesting – just at dawn and dusk. But if she dies or disappears, he starts all-day song again to find another mate.

British robins and tawny owls are resident birds, staying in Britain all year. They need to defend a territory throughout the year to ensure they have a place to find food, so they sing all year. The females sing too.

Bird song varies through the day. It is at its peak in the dawn chorus, just after the first glimmer of morning light. Birds seem to warm up to a peak of sound that lasts about an hour. They don't all start singing at the same time. Species that eat insects and worms start earlier than seed-eaters.

Birds sing through the early morning, go quiet around mid-day and sing a bit in the afternoon. There is another peak of song in the evening before they go to roost, but this is quieter than the dawn chorus.

Weather also affects bird song. Birds sing more in warm weather and less in cold or windy weather. However, mistle thrushes sing from the tops of trees and buildings into the teeth of a gale and are sometimes called 'storm cocks'.

Bird calls are important too. Calls are simple notes produced by males and females all year round: they are birds' day-to-day conversation. They call to keep in touch with others, to signal danger and when raising young. Some have many different calls (chaffinches have 15) but others have one or two.

Pairs of gannets clatter their bills together to show each other that they are not aggressive and to reinforce the bond between them.

There are two kinds of calls: contact calls and breeding calls. Contact calls help to keep flocks of birds together. Songbirds moving through a wood in a small flock make little 'chip' or 'tack' noises. There may be several bird species feeding in a mixed finch flock in winter, but they will make similar contact calls that all understand.

Breeding calls must be unique to individuals. A young bird must know its parent's 'voice' from those of other adult birds, especially in breeding colonies where birds live close together.

Gannets nest close together out of beak's reach from each other. They call when they land and to greet their mate. Landing birds are ignored unless they land in the wrong place. Calling saves the landing bird from being attacked by its mate on the nest.

Calling also helps a returning bird find its mate in the colony. Manx shearwaters use the same island nesting burrow year after year. Males arrive first and when a female arrives, she calls for her mate. She will recognise the answering call of her mate from the year before and use the sound of his call to locate the burrow.

Guillemot chicks call to their parents from inside the egg. The parents know each chick's voice even before they hatch. This is important as the adult leads the chicks from the ledge to the water.

The mother of this fledgling robin knows its call from that of other birds and will respond to it.

Alarm calls warn other birds of danger. 'Chat' alarms are noisy and warn of an approaching cat. This noise ensures the cat will not surprise its prey. A thin, 'seep' call – often from deep in a bush – is made when a bird of prey flies overhead.

Birds also produce other sounds. Male prairie chickens have a pouch in their neck which they pump up with air and use like bellows to make popping calls. Woodpeckers tap trees with their beaks to make loud 'drumming' noises that echo in woodland. Snipes make a bleating sound using special tail feathers that vibrate during their display flight.

SOCIAL LIFE

Birds of many species gather in flocks. Sometimes these are flocks of one species only; sometimes they are mixed flocks. Birds flock to feed, to roost, or simply to fly together. There are advantages to being with other birds, but there are also disadvantages. Without a few rules of behaviour, a flock could be an unruly free-for-all. Flocking birds of all kinds behave in a way that ensures each bird benefits from belonging.

It is important for birds to keep their distance in a flock. This helps ensure that they don't collide in the air and helps prevent squabbles over food and territory. Some species are more sociable than others and are comfortable closer together. Other birds keep much further apart to avoid trouble. If a bird gets too close, a jab of the bill or a display of aggression will follow – watch how swallows behave on a wire! Herons keep several meters away from each other, but bee-eaters are so sociable that they huddle close together.

Birds keep their distance when feeding to ensure that each bird has a patch in which to feed. Starlings space themselves out when probing garden lawns for beetle larvae. When there is plenty of food, they feed closer together. Wood pigeons will gather in a flock to feed on a pile of grain and tits may gather at bird tables if there is plenty to eat.

Birds that feed together regularly have a 'pecking order' in the flock. The pecking order is the right of one bird to eat or choose its roosting place before another. In a flock that stays together, each bird knows its place. This ensures the well-being of the flock as a whole. But in hard times, the strongest birds will survive while those lower in the ranks may starve. In this way the fittest survive and the flock stays healthy.

In late afternoon, starlings gather in a big, noisy group at a meeting point before flocking to their night-time roost.

Male ruffs display for a living and have more showy plumage than the females. They compete with each other for females in a special display area called a 'lek'.

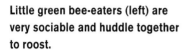

Little green bee-eaters (left) are very sociable and huddle together to roost.

At night, most birds find somewhere to perch and rest safely. Some birds roost in their nests, while others make a special nest just for roosting. Treecreepers hide in cavities under bark. Wrens make a roosting nest or use nestboxes, other birds' nests or other cavities.

Birds that feed in flocks tend to roost in flocks. Sheltered roosts help keep birds warm in winter especially if there are several huddled together. They share their body heat and save energy. Wrens, swifts and treecreepers all do this. Staying close together means that there are less of their bodies in contact with cold air and so less body heat is lost.

Robins feed on their own but may leave their winter territories to roost with other robins. Some roosts are huge, containing millions of birds!

Being in a group also makes it less likely that an individual will be attacked by a predator. Although large roosts are a bigger target for predators, it is worth the risk because there are more eyes and ears to be on the look-out for danger. The birds on the edge of the group are at greater risk. These birds are low in the pecking order.

Studies of a merlin hunting wader flocks in winter showed that a wader was three times more likely to be caught when it was on its own than in a flock.

Roosting birds may somehow also pass on information about good places to feed. Birds gather in roosts from a wide area and those that have fed well may behave differently to those that have not fed well. Hungry birds may then follow well-fed birds to a better feeding place.

Territory

The patch one bird defends from another is called a territory. A starling's territory can be a small nest hole whereas a golden eagle's territory can cover a vast area.

Birds may hold territories for a few minutes or for several years. They use them as places to attract a mate, to nest or to feed. Woodpeckers and birds of prey pair up, nest and feed all in one territory. Swallows and waterbirds court and nest in their territory, but move around to feed. This is because they cannot defend an area of water or air

Roosting mallards peek every now and then to check all around is safe. Birds on the edge of the group peek more often than those further in, which are safer from danger.

where they feed. Oystercatchers have two territories: one on land where they court and nest and a separate feeding territory along the shore. Robins and wrens defend winter feeding territories.

For most male birds to breed, they must first hold a territory. Great tits need a territory with a suitable nesting hole. Ground-nesting birds will look for a mound to perch on. Nectar-feeding birds, such as sunbirds, need plenty of the right flowers to supply nectar.

Any territory must be large enough to supply a bird's needs. In winter, pied wagtails will defend a stretch of riverbank where they can feed on dead insects washed up on the bank. If there is plenty of food, they won't waste time by chasing away wrens and robins. But, if food is scarce, any invading birds will be chased away. When the territory can no longer supply enough food, pied wagtails gather to forage in small flocks. Sometimes another wagtail will be allowed to share the food of one territory in return for helping to chase away other invaders.

A hummingbird moves around its territory, drinking from flowers in turn. Each flower quickly renews its stock of nectar. But birds which eat fruit, use up their food supply. When mistle thrushes have stripped a tree of its berries, they must move to another. By eating different types of berries, there is always something for them to eat.

In most birds pairs, the male sets up a territory at the start of the breeding season and noisily defends it. Once territories are established, the paired-up birds settle down to breed. Because the black-browed albatross and the mute swan live a long time and pair for life, they use the same territory year after year.

Birds are busy defending their territories at the start of the season. Once birds know each others' territories, things quieten down as they get on with breeding. Squabbling is most common where lots of birds live close together. Colonies of nesting birds are some of the noisiest places you can imagine, with arguments over territory a common event.

Life in a colony

One in 10 of all bird species breeds in colonies. Some colonies, such as seabird nesting cliffs are densely packed with birds:

An emperor penguin colony.

Gannets nest in colonies on rocky stacks, cliff-ledges and slopes around the British coastline. The colony is noisy with the sound of birds jealously defending their nests and chicks.

others are more spaced out. Living in a colony has some of the same advantages as being part of a roost. Birds follow each other to the best feeding areas and there is more protection from predators. But colonies also attract predators. This is why they are often tucked away on islands, cliffs or sandbars to deter animals such as foxes and rats.

Some species nest in colonies in certain conditions. Eiders (a species of duck) nest together on islands but nest alone on the mainland where they use their camouflaged plumage to hide themselves from predators.

Nesting in a crowd has its problems as territorial birds living together are aggressive. If they nest just out of reach of each other, the problem is partly solved. Displays take the place of aggression. Diseases are probably more easily spread where birds live together closely. Nest material can be stolen and unguarded eggs and nests can be evicted.

In densely packed colonies, male birds must spend more time defending their mates and protecting their eggs and chicks from attack. Aggression is worse the closer the birds have to nest to each other. Displays are used instead of fighting – they say the same thing to a rival without a fight, which could harm both birds.

FINDING A MATE

A bird must mate to make sure that there is a next generation of its own kind. To find a suitable partner, the male advertises by displays, songs and calls. He may not be able to attract a mate until he has his own territory.

Birds are wary of each other, so they use courtship rituals to overcome their urge to attack each other. One ritual is courtship feeding. Males of many birds feed their females to provide her with the extra food she needs when her body is making eggs or when she is incubating and cannot leave the nest. Male birds of prey feed their mates while they sit on the eggs so they do not have to leave the nest unguarded, whereas female hummingbirds feed the males while they incubate the eggs.

Another ritual is called 'allopreening' where birds in a pair preen each others feathers. Herons, crows, pigeons and many other birds do this. They usually preen the feathers that are difficult to reach and it helps to cement their bond.

Staying together

Most birds stay with their chosen partner throughout the breeding season. Except for a very few animals (the duck-billed platypus is one), birds are the only warm-blooded animals to lay eggs. It takes lots of energy to make eggs and rear a family and it's too much work for one bird, so it makes sense for them to pair up. Pairs in different species share the task in different ways.

The male chaffinch, for example, follows his mate while she builds the nest but he does not help. He also leaves her to sit on the eggs. He does not feed her but he goes with her when she looks for food. When the eggs hatch, however, he helps to raise the young.

In many bird species, the male shares all the tasks equally with his mate. Breeding is harder work for females than for males, so she must take her time to choose the right mate. The male will display and the female will choose her partner by how he behaves.

Female weaverbirds choose their mate for their skills at building a nest that will not fall apart in the rainy season! When he has made it, she inspects it and if she likes it, she lines it with soft grass, mates and lays her eggs.

Other mates are chosen for their skills in finding food. Male terns offer fish to their mates as part of courtship. When the female is forming eggs

inside her body, she stays still and the male feeds her. He carries on feeding her until the young are growing strong. If he is skilful, the family has a good start in life.

Some birds, such as black-headed gulls, mate soon after they have displayed; others take their time. Albatrosses pair one year or more before mating and laying eggs. In pairs where males and females are loyal to each other (called 'monogomy'), the male often guards his mate or defends his territory from other males. Fulmars, gulls, geese, swans and gannets all do this.

Kittiwakes spend winter at sea. At the start of the breeding season they return to their cliff ledges to breed. Older birds arrive first in February, and are followed by less experienced birds. First-time breeders arrive even later in April or May. The older birds pair up and the young birds are left with each other. The older birds do better because they have more experience and because they start earlier in the season. If breeding is successful, the pair will stay together. But if it isn't, they are likely to seek new partners and try again.

Moorhens are unusual because it is the female that takes the lead. Moorhens live in small flocks in winter. They pair up before finding a territory and the female fights off other females.

A male that has a successful female will defend her from the attentions of other males. After all, he has wasted his time if another male comes along and fertilises his mate's eggs. Male ducks, finches and swallows keep close to their mates while they are forming eggs. They want to ensure that their sperm fertilises the eggs and so they

Mating can be a dangerous business. Female Canada geese are sometimes drowned by over-enthusiastic males who hold them under the water (left).

Bowerbirds such as this male (right) specialise in display. He attracts his mate by making a spectacular bower to impress her.

will follow the females around to make sure that other males do not mate with their partners.

A male can defend his mate against another male, but a group of males can overcome him. A 'gang' of mallards sometimes forces a female to mate. This is called 'cuckoldry' and sometimes it nearly drowns the female. One in 10 mallard ducklings is the result of cuckoldry.

Most birds choose one mate only. But one in 10 bird species regularly mates with several birds. Having more than one mate is called 'polygamy'.

It is more common for a male to mate with two or more females (called 'polygyny'), but in a few cases, a female will have more than one male partner This is called 'polyandry'.

The male ruff does nothing to help rear his young. He does not defend a nest or a female, but he does defend a patch of ground where he can mate. His aim is to mate with as many females as he can and he competes with other males for the right to mate with several females. Competition is intense as male ruffs put all their energy into displaying. A male ruff's plumage is much more colourful than that of the drab, brown female.

Competition between males for females takes place at traditional display ground called a 'lek' and each male has a 'court' around him. Dominant males may share a court with a younger 'satellite' male that

The male northern jacana incubates the eggs and rears the young alone.

hangs around. He can be identified by his white ruff of feathers. Dominant males may be too busy fighting off other males to notice the satellite male mating with a female!

Red-legged partridges share the task of rearing a family. But if there's enough food, the female lays a second clutch of eggs, leaving her mate to look after the first clutch so that she can sit on the second clutch herself.

The northern jacana, found from Texas to Costa Rica, is the only species in which the female is known to have several males at any one time. A female may have two or three males that have built floating nests in her watery territory. Each male fertilises her eggs, which she lays in his nest. She then leaves him to rear the young, but will help him to drive away predators.

The bright female red-necked phalarope guards her drab mate from other females.

Like ruffs, male black grouse also compete for females at a traditional display ground or 'lek'. Instead of displaying a ruff of feathers, they spread their wings and tails.

Birds of paradise and bowerbirds are among the most beautiful of all creatures. The males play no part in caring and rearing the family, but devote their energies to elaborate display and courtship rituals. Males have 'courts' where they can show off to the best advantage. Females visit the courts, choose a male, are courted, mate and then leave.

Instead of having spectacular plumage, male bowerbirds put all their efforts into making an impressive court of leaves on the forest floor. It's the court that impresses the female, so he doesn't need to look smart!

The dunnock (or hedge sparrow) has a very complicated love life! Males set up territories in spring and, later on, females set up feeding ranges – a kind of territory where they search for food. If a female's feeding range is in the territory of one male, she will mate with him. But if her range overlaps with the territories of two males, she will mate with both males and they will help her to feed the chicks.

However, the situation is more complicated than that. A male may share his territory with a smaller, less dominant male. The number one male will guard the female when

A male dunnock may share his territory with another male.

she is about to lay her eggs. To do this, he may have to spend much of this time chasing the number two male away. Fights can break out and the number two male may be killed, but there is a chance that number two will get to mate with the female.

As it is in the number one male's best interests to be the father of the chicks, he tries to improve his chances. Just before mating, he pecks at the female's cloaca. She responds by pushing out sperm stored from other matings. When number one mates with her, his sperm replaces those of his rivals. But, because the number two male has mated with the female, he will also help to rear the young.

Long-lived birds tend to be more loyal to each other. Mute swans mate for life. Older, more experienced pairs make better parents.

RAISING A FAMILY

Birds care for their young and this care starts with laying and incubating eggs. They must be kept at the right temperature, so the chick inside grows quickly. The quicker the chicks hatch, the less time a predator will have to take them. Newly hatched chicks depend on their parents and most parents care for their young until they fly.

Nests

A few birds make no nest at all, but most make a nest to keep eggs warm, together and safe from danger. Nests can be simple or very fancy: from a simple scrape in the ground used by waders, to the finely woven nests of weaverbirds. Nesting above ground gives safety from many predators. Eagles and ospreys build a massive nest from piles of sticks and use it each year. Most birds build with stems, leaves, moss and twigs. Swallows make cup-like nests with mud and water. Swifts use spit as cement, working it with their feet. In the tropics, where snakes like eggs, many birds build nests with a roof. Birds that nest in holes and cavities include kingfishers, tits and parrots. Kingfishers

A female ringed plover pretends to be injured. She makes herself obvious to distract a predator away from her nearby nest.

lay their eggs on the cavity floor. Treecreepers nest behind loose bark; puffins use burrows – sometimes rabbit holes – in the ground.

After mating, a female can store sperm in her body, but usually lays eggs a day later. She lays enough eggs to produce the most young the parents can care for. Birds of prey lay more eggs when there is plenty of food, but may not breed at all during hard times.

Care of eggs

Laying stops when incubation starts. For most birds, incubation means sitting on the eggs to keep them just at the right temperature for the young to grow strong quickly. If the eggs are too warm or too cool, the embryos will die. While on the nest, the adults are vulnerable to attack and use energy while incubating. Male and female kestrels share incubation. In birds of prey, the female incubates and the male feeds her. Cormorants, gannets and other web-footed birds incubate their eggs with their feet. Most birds have a brood patch – special loose, bare skin on their breasts that they lower over the eggs. The sitting bird turns the eggs to make sure all are warmed and the right way up.

In hot countries, eggs must

A great skua or 'bonxie' warns a walker he's too near its nest by dive bombing him in flight.

The fairy tern doesn't build a nest but balances her single egg on a branch.

Nestboxes in gardens are popular nesting places for blue tits.

be prevented from cooking! Desert birds shield eggs from the sun – the adults pant and spread their wings. Sandgrouse soak their breast feathers in water and use them like a sponge to cool the eggs and young.

Parents must defend their nests carefully. A safe nesting place is a good start. Some birds nest near a more dangerous animal for protection. Sparrows nest in the big stick piles that ospreys make. Weavers and wrens nest near bees' and wasps' nests for protection.

Adult ground-nesting birds are often camouflaged so they hide against the ground when they are still. Females that incubate are drabber than males so as not to stand out. Terns and gulls lure predators away from their nests by distracting them with display.

Male weaverbirds weave elaborate basket-like nests which are suspended from trees for safety.

Some birds use their surroundings to incubate their eggs. One group of birds specialises in finding or making natural incubators for their eggs and they do not use their bodies at all. They are ground-dwelling game birds of the megapode family and they live in Australia, New Guinea and Indonesia.

The mallee fowl lives in dry scrub and is the champion of incubator birds. It builds a compost pit of leaves in the ground and covers it with sand to keep in heat. The eggs are laid in a chamber near to the surface and the male checks the temperature of the heap over the following months, opening and closing it to make sure that it is just right!

The male emperor penguin incubates one egg on his feet for 64 days!

Care of young

Some birds are very well-grown when they hatch and leave the nest very soon after hatching. These are 'nest-fleeing' birds and they start to call even before they hatch to build a strong bond with their parents.

Other birds are helpless when newly hatched. These nest in hide-away places and tend to be born naked with their eyes closed. They are fed by their parents and stay in the nest until almost fully grown.

Parent birds must warm their young chicks with their bodies until they are big enough and have the right feathers to keep warm on their own. A spell of cold or wet weather can be disastrous for chicks – it makes food hard to find and, because it is colder, parents have to spend more time keeping their young warm and so they have less time to feed.

Parents of helpless young will remove their nestlings' droppings. Woodpeckers and song-birds produce a sac with droppings in, which the parents eat or remove. This helps to prevent disease, keeps the nest dry and clean and removes signs of nesting, which could be spotted by a predator.

Helpless young are fed by their parents. Parent pied flycatchers visit their nests 30 times an hour and they make more than 6000 trips to rear each brood.

Feeding takes place during daylight hours. As there is more daylight in the Arctic in summer, snow buntings can feed their young by day and night.

Birds of prey rip and tear their prey into pieces to feed to their young. Garden warblers and other songbirds push their catch of insects into the wide open mouths (gapes) of their nestlings.

When they are hungry, helpless chicks beg for good by stretching up with their mouths open. Begging calls and gaping mouths are a signal to the parents to feed their young. The lining of a chick's mouth is often brightly coloured to make it a clear target for the adult bringing food to it.

When there is plenty of food around, chicks are fed in turn, but when there's a shortage, some go hungry and may even die. Some birds, such as owls, birds of prey, swifts and herons, give the oldest chicks the best treatment. Older owl nestlings will survive at the expense of younger ones. If there is plenty of food, all of the chicks will survive; if there is a shortage, the youngest will die.

Grebes and swans will carry their young on their backs. Water rails, moorhens and other birds have been recorded flying with a chick clasped between their feet!

Fully grown moorhen chicks from the first brood help the adults feed a second brood of young.

Tawny owls continue to feed their chicks after they have left the nest. The downy young are able to walk about before they can fly and they call to be fed.

Help from others

In one-third of the world's bird species, parents are helped by other adult birds to rear their young. Most of these birds live in tropical or semi-tropical places. But a few species live in cooler countries.

In moorhens, fledglings from the first brood of the season will help to feed the young of the second brood. Long-tailed tits may be helped by other adults who have lost their nest. Raising a family is hard work for parents and it is dangerous. It makes sense for parent birds to rear their young as quickly as possible so there is less time when they are vulnerable to attack and so the adults can get back into shape and rear a second brood.

Some birds use crèches to look after their young. Groups of young shelducks gather into crèches of sometimes more than 100 ducklings with a few adults. It is thought that predators are less likely to attack such big groups. Eider ducklings also gather in crèches with 'aunties', adult female eiders, to look after them. The young ducks may be snatched by large gulls.

Big groups of well-grown tern, penguin and pelican chicks gather together to protect themselves from predators while the adults continue to feed them. Large groups of emperor penguin chicks huddle together for warmth in the icy climate of Antarctica.

The cuckoo plays no part in the care of its chicks at all. It leaves the task to a foster parent (like this reed warbler), in whose nest it has laid its egg. When the cuckoo chick hatches, it throws any other eggs or young out of the nest, so the parents have just one large chick to feed!

MIGRATION

Migration has fascinated scientists for centuries. People have written books all about migration. Today we know much more than ever about migration, but we still do not know how a bird finds its way to its destination.

Migration is usually used to describe regular journeys between two areas. They are usually journeys over land but, in some cases they are vertical (up and down) from mountain tops to coastal areas.

In Britain and in temperate Europe and America, migrant birds 'fly south for the winter'. But ringing has revealed that this is only part of the story. Sometimes, not all the birds migrate and the migration is said to be partial. Blackcaps, for example, are summer migrants, but a few stay in Britain for the winter. In Sweden, female chaffinches migrate south, but the males stay for winter.

Birds probably migrate for two reasons: to avoid harsh conditions such as winter or drought, and when food or water is hard to find, or to go where there is less competition for food and nesting places. A good food supply is vital for all birds.

Short winter days and long, cold dark nights make finding food difficult. Keeping warm is also a problem in winter. Geese and waders breed in the Arctic, but frozen conditions mean that they have to leave before winter. Some birds, like the ptarmigan, can survive these conditions. They dig roots from under the snow and they make snow hollows to shelter in.

Swallows gather on telegraph wires before making the autumn migration to south of the Sahara desert.

When it's too cold to support flying insects, swifts, martins, swallows and flycatchers must go in search of warmer climes where insects are plentiful. We think of swallows coming 'home' to breed, but they spend more of their time in Africa than here.

So how does a bird start a migratory lifestyle? Take the serin, for example. About 100 years ago, the serin was a Mediterranean bird. Then it began to spread northwards and has now reached southern Sweden. In the Mediterranean it doesn't migrate, but in the north of its range, it must migrate in winter.

As well as regular migrations, changes in the weather can make birds move. Many birds from continental Europe spend the winter in Britain, where it is milder. But if it is cold here, they'll move on to even milder places. Ducks, thrushes, waders and finches will all do this.

When a berry, fruit or seed crop fails, huge numbers of birds must up and move to a new supply. This is called an 'irruption'. Crossbills that feed on conifer seeds, waxwings that eat berries, and siskins that eat birch and alder seeds all irrupt.

Jays irrupt in northern Europe: in 1983 when the acorn crop failed, flocks of jays (normally shy, solitary birds) arrived on the English coastline.

Long distance travellers

It is truly amazing that tiny creatures can travel so far. The Arctic tern nests in the Arctic and migrates a total of 18,000 kilometers (11,000 miles) to the Antarctic. It sees more daylight than any other animal! But unlike many migrants, it can feed during its journey – it must, or it would die. Others cannot stop to feed. The tiny ruby-throated hummingbird flies a non-stop 1,000 km (600 miles) across the Gulf of Mexico in 24 hours, without food.

Non-stop flight uses up lots of energy. Birds must fuel themselves with fat – they have to feed up before migrating. They prepare to migrate when there's lots of food around, and the migration takes them to where they won't go short of food.

To migrate, it's best to be about the size of a large wader – not too heavy, but big and powerful enough to press on against the wind. Migrating warblers have longer and narrower wings than those that don't. They are better for long sustained flights. Small birds migrate with a bounding flight; rise and fall, glide and flap. It saves energy. Big birds such as storks, herons and large birds of prey soar using currents of warm air called thermals, which give them lift and help them save energy in flight.

These warm currents of air form only over land and not over sea, so big birds that have to cross the sea do so at the warmest – and narrowest – point.

Those that cross sea have to keep on going. Many birds prefer to migrate at night – rails, owls, nightjars, warblers and thrushes are all night-fliers. Flying by night means that they don't get too hot, and they are safer from predators.

Birds prefer to migrate in fair weather. Strong winds may blow them off-course (much to the delight of birdwatchers who can predict a 'fall' of migrants by reading the weather).

If you'd like to find out more about migration, there's a book in this series called *Migrants and Migration*, by Peter Holden.

During its lifetime, the Arctic tern sees more daylight than any other animal.

COPING WITH EXTREMES

Harsh conditions present many challenges for birds, which have evolved some ingenious ways to survive.

Too hot and dry

Desert birds can last a long time without drinking: their bodies save water. Unlike other animals, birds don't sweat; they cool themselves by panting or by fluttering the bare skin in the pouch under their chins to lose heat. Birds can allow their body temperatures to rise higher than most animals could cope with so that they do not lose precious water from their bodies while cooling down.

Many birds have evolved special adaptations to cope with these conditions. Male sandgrouse, for example, wade into water to soak their breast feathers which act like a sponge. They then fly to their nests where the chicks drink by sucking the moist feathers.

Too salty

Most creatures cannot drink salt water because it makes their blood salty. Birds that live in salt marshes, desert or marine habitats have to remove salt in different ways. Seabirds and flamingos have special glands above the eyes which release salty droplets. Some birds shake them off – petrels spray them away! Wading birds that feed in salty estuaries may have to cope with water that gets saltier as the tides change.

Too small

Small birds have a special problem. Because their bodies are big on the outside compared to the amount of flesh they have inside, they

Up to 50 wrens have been known to roost in a single nestbox in winter!

heat up very quickly when it's hot and cool down very quickly when it's cold. Keeping warm and keeping cool are real problems for small birds and they do it in different ways. Small birds often flock together and roost together, especially in winter. Wrens, for example, huddle together in night-time roosts to share their body warmth. Up to 50 or more birds have been known to shelter in a single nestbox to roost.

Too cold

When snow covers the ground, hunters may have difficulty seeing their prey. Many owls hunt by the day during winter. Frost makes the ground rock-hard which means that birds that probe for their food may go hungry. Frozen ground presents a big problem for woodcocks, which probe for worms and other creatures in damp woodland soil.

Birds can fly away from these areas. In very cold weather, some birds move to avoid starving. Many inland kingfishers die during harsh winters; those near the coast are

In winter, the ptarmigan's mottled feathers turn snow-white for camouflage and it even has feathery feet as white winter boots!

The grey gull nests in the Atacama Desert, Chile. It's the driest place on Earth and adults must fly 30 km to sea to feed. At night, they bring food to their chicks.

luckier – they move to the seaside when rivers and lakes freeze. Open country feeders such as lapwings, thrushes and skylarks also move to find food. Some birds move into built-up areas: the air in towns and cities is much warmer than the surrounding countryside in winter.

FURTHER READING AND ADDRESSES

The YOC is the club to join to find out more about birds, other wildlife and the environment – it's the junior membership of The Royal Society for the Protection of Birds. YOC members receive a bi-monthly, full-colour magazine full of fascinating information, plus quizzes, competitions, holidays and lots more to do. Write to: YOC, The Lodge, Sandy, Bedfordshire SG19 2DL to find out more.

Birdwatch and *Bird Watching* magazines are colourful magazines about birds and bird-watching. Both are available from good newsagents. *BBC Wildlife* magazine covers all wildlife, with some news and features about birds.

Some good books to buy, or borrow from your local library:

The Birdwatchers' Yearbook (published annually by Buckingham Press: ISBN 0 951 49655 7). Lists everything from county bird recorders to bird observatories, plus articles.

Bird Behaviour by Robert Burton (Granada, 1985: ISBN 0 246 12440 7). This is a big book for older readers and is full of superb colour photographs and fascinating facts about birds and what they do.

The other three titles in the Hamlyn Young Ornithologist's Guide series are *Bird Identification and Fieldcraft*, *Migrants and Migration* and *Bird Habitats and Conservation*. These fascinating books introduce readers to the world of birds and birdwatching.

INDEX

O

oil, preen 11
oilbird 17, 21
osprey 25, 38, 39
ostrich 13, 20, 45
owls 11, 15, 16, 28, 40, 41, 43, 44
oxygen 8
oystercatcher 23, 32

P

panting 44
parasites 12
parrots 11, 15, 21, 38
partridges 36
peacock 26
pecking order 19, 25, 30
pelican, white 19, 41
penguins 9, 23, 39, 41
peregrine 9, 24
petrels 15, 23, 44,
phalaropes 24, 36
pheasants 10, 12, 27
pigeons 20, 30, 34
pirates 25
plant-eaters 20
plovers 18, 23, 38
prairie chickens 29
predators 8, 9, 16, 24, 31, 33, 41
preening 10, 11
prey 24
ptarmigan 42, 45
puffin 13, 25

R

rail 40, 43
razorbill 13
reptile 10
rhea 9
ringing 42

robin 12, 14, 16, 17, 19, 26, 28, 29, 31, 32
rook 12
roosting 7, 31, 44
ruff 31, 36

S

saltmarsh 44
sandgrouse 12, 39, 44
sandpipers 23
sawbills 22
scavengers 24, 25
scoter 22
seabirds 6, 23, 44
seed-eaters 20, 43
senses 14, 15
serin 42
shearwaters 15, 16, 19, 29
shelduck 41
shoveler 19, 22
siskin 43
skimmers 23
skuas 25, 39
skylark 45
smew 22
snipe 29
song and songs 15, 16, 26, 27, 28
songbirds 27, 40
sparrowhawk 9, 19, 24
sparrows 12, 39
squabbling 32
starlings 6, 25, 30, 31
stealing, milk 14
    food 25
stilts 23
stork 22, 23, 43
sunbathing 11, 12
sunbirds 21
swallows 11, 21, 30, 31, 35, 42
swans 8, 11, 20, 32, 35, 36, 40

swiflet, cave 17
swifts 11, 16, 21, 31, 38, 42
swimming 13

T

teal (see also ducks) 27
terns 34, 39, 43
territory 31, 34
thermals 43
thrushes 28 32, 43, 45
tits 12, 14, 18, 20, 21, 32, 38, 41
toucan 21
treecreeper 12, 13, 31, 38
turnstone 24

U

ultra-violet light 14
umbrella bird 22

V

vision (see also eyes, nocturnal birds) 14, 17
vultures 24, 25

W

wading birds 23, 24, 38, 42, 43, 44
wagtails 12, 32
walking 12
warblers 21, 27, 40, 43
waterbirds 22, 31
waterproofing 10, 11
weather 24, 28, 43
weaverbirds 34, 38, 39
woodcock 15, 16, 24, 45
woodpeckers 12, 13, 19, 22, 29, 31, 40
woodpecker finch 14

The photographs are copyright and are reproduced by kind permission of:

p.4 Bill Oddie; p.5 Roger Tidman; p.9 Hugh Clark (Nature Photographers Ltd); p.10 Mark Hamblin (RSPB); p.13 Owen Newman (Nature Photographers Ltd); p.14/15 Michael W Powles (Aquila); p.17 J Markham (Bruce Coleman Ltd); p.19 Michael Gore (Nature Photographers Ltd); p.21 Roger Tidman (Nature Photographers Ltd); p.23 R T Smith (RSPB); p.25 C H Gomersall (RSPB); p.27 G Downey (RSPB); p.29 Paul Sterry (Nature Photographers Ltd); p.31 Gunter Ziesler (Bruce Coleman Ltd); p.33 Roger Tidman; p.35 (left) C H Gomersall (RSPB); p.35 (right) Kevin Carlson (Nature Photographers Ltd); p.36 Philip J Newman (RSPB); p.39 G Reddick (Aquila); p.40, 41 Roger Wilmshurst (RSPB); p.45 Wayne Lankinen (Aquila).